Unleashing Potential

Unleashing Potential

Embracing the Power of a Growth Mindset

Philip M. Baker

Reimagining Life Coaches
Marana, AZ

ISBN: E-book- 979-8-218-26078-1
Paperback- 979-8-218-26139-9

Cover Designer: Philip M. Baker
Editor: Deborah A. Gaston

Published by Reimagining Life Coaches
Marana, AZ

For more information:
 email: philip@reimagininglifecoaches.com
or visit   www.reimagininglifecoaches.com

Table Of Contents

Dedication

To My Dearest Wife,
Thank you for being my unwavering pillar of support, my rock through the highs and lows of life. Your love, encouragement, and belief in me have been the fuel that propels me forward, making the journey of growth and achievement all the more rewarding. Your unwavering presence and understanding have brought light to my darkest days, and I am endlessly grateful for the warmth and love you bring into my life.

To My Loving Family and Friends,
Your unwavering encouragement and belief in my dreams have been a constant source of inspiration. Your cheering voices, guiding hands, and unyielding support have lifted me when I needed it the most. Each of you has played an instrumental role in shaping the person I am today, and I cherish the memories we have created together. This book is a testament to the love and encouragement you have showered upon me, and I dedicate its pages to each of you.

To God,
I humbly thank You for trusting me with the precious gift of creativity. Your divine touch has instilled in me the passion, drive, and desire to use this gift to change lives beyond my own. Your guidance and presence

have been a constant source of strength, reminding me that I am never alone on this journey. I dedicate this work to You, acknowledging that every word penned and every idea conceived reflect the boundless creativity You have blessed me with. This book is an offering of my gratitude and a testimony of Your incredible love, power, and inspiration.

Foreword

"Beloved, I pray that all may go well with you and that you may be in good health, just as it is well with your soul."

3 John 1:2 NRSV

"Stay alert. This is hazardous work I'm assigning you. You're going to be like sheep running through a wolf pack, so don't call attention to yourselves. Be as cunning as a snake, inoffensive as a dove."

Matthew 10:16 (The Message)

"Give yourself permission to question certainties you once bet your life on."

Poet Jeanne Lohmann

Recent years have left many of us feeling troubled, tentative, and uncertain about ourselves and our world. Where do we fit in? What do we have to offer? These questions may feel haunting even as we desire to take steps to change our trajectory toward living a full life.

While these are uncertain times, they are also compelling times. So much seems to be needed all around us! The world is changing fast, and people's needs are too. How and where to get involved, to bring our most whole selves, and to be fully present seems like a clarion call.

Philip Baker has an extensive career encouraging growth and development in those around him. He was coaching before "life coaching" had a definition in the public arena. Philip worked in nonprofit organizations where he was responsible for advocating for fathers in court and facilitating weekly interaction and instruction periods as mandated by the court system. This effort was to help them learn to be more responsible parents so they could regain access to their children's lives. His work with The Fatherhood Project led to the creation of ABBA Fathers (Authentic Building Blocks of Accountability for Fathers)—an organization he founded using the Bible to clarify a father's responsibilities. He created this online group to connect, inform, and share insights with fathers on the responsibility to replicate rather than just duplicate children, especially sons. ABBA Fathers grew an international following of men seeking to improve their parenting skills and interactions with their children.

Philip has worked in ministry, music ministry, leadership development, and diverse settings of personal growth development. As he began working with mindfulness and mindsets, he discovered that it resonated with his own belief in God as well as his experiences and expertise. He brings a wise, deep, and faithful desire to marketplace ministry in this season of his life.

In *Unleashing Potential: Embracing the Power of a Growth Mindset*, Philip offers readers a compelling exploration of how mindsets influence beliefs. He suggests that readers consider mindsets and how their beliefs about themselves influence abilities, decisions, potentials, and the nature of forward momentum. He provides insightful reflection on the how-to of challenging mindsets and limiting beliefs.

Philip also offers strategies for shifting mindsets through intentional practices.

Philip's book is filled with information, insights, and encouragement that can help the reader discover new understandings of themselves and how to implement learning. He brings together mindfulness and mindsets in a way that supports the individual, family, or workplace in growing forward during this disruptive time in the world.

Unleashing Potential is a book to be read with a highlighter, journal, and pen in hand. This book is rich with insight, information, and education about mindsets and mindfulness. Fostering your own growth-oriented identity, curiosity, and resilience will enable you to move through this season of transition, growth, change, and professional development with an eye on leveraging what you know and learn, cultivating gratitude, and embracing wholeness.

Deborah Brandt, Watershed Moments Coaching

Preface

Welcome to *Unleashing Potential: Embracing the Power of a Growth Mindset*. In the following pages, you are about to embark on a journey of self-discovery, transformation, and empowerment. This book delves into the profound influence of mindsets on our lives, illuminating the stark contrast between a fixed mindset and a growth mindset.

You might be wondering why I should be the one writing this book, and my reply is, why not me? You see, I had my own personal journey of transformation and renewal of my mindset that led me to create and succeed at the goals I set for myself and to tremendous growth. I felt I couldn't keep this to myself, knowing others needed it like I did. I became a Life Coach for this very reason.

Throughout this book, you'll find a plethora of insights drawn from psychology, neuroscience, education, and personal anecdotes. The pages are carefully crafted to guide you through self-awareness and introspection, enabling you to recognize your current mindset, challenge its limitations, and embrace the power of growth. From the science that explains the malleability of intelligence to the practical strategies for fostering a growth-oriented environment, each chapter is designed to empower you to take control of your mindset and chart a course toward fulfilling your aspirations.

Remember that this journey is not just about information; it is about your transformation. The words on these pages are meant to inspire action and invite reflection. Whether you're seeking personal growth, aiming to enhance your relationships, or pursuing professional success, the principles of a growth mindset have the potential to reshape your trajectory. The stories shared, and the research explored aim to empower the reader to tap into their limitless potential.

Your mindset is the compass that guides your choices, shapes your outcomes, and determines your perception of the world around you. With an open heart and a willingness to explore the depths of your beliefs, you can redefine your narrative, rewrite your story, and unlock the doors to a life enriched by growth, resilience, and boundless possibilities.

Warmly,

Philip M. Baker

Chapter 1

Introduction: The Power of Mindsets

Part 1: Unlocking Growth and Transformation

In this modern age of rapid change and evolving opportunities, our mindset plays a crucial role in determining our success, fulfillment, and personal growth. Our beliefs, attitudes, and perspectives shape how we approach challenges, handle setbacks, and strive for achievement. Two contrasting mindsets that significantly impact our lives are the fixed mindset and the growth mindset.

Understanding Mindsets

A mindset can be defined as a set of deeply ingrained beliefs and assumptions that influence how we perceive ourselves and the world around us. It is the lens through which we interpret and respond to various situations and experiences. Our mindset shapes our thoughts, emotions, and behaviors, ultimately determining the outcomes we achieve.

The *fixed mindset* is characterized by a belief that our abilities, intelligence, and talents are fixed traits that cannot be significantly developed. Individuals with a fixed mindset tend to believe their qualities are inherent and unchangeable, leading them to perceive challenges, failures, and criticism as personal reflections of their limitations. They often seek validation by demonstrating their abilities effortlessly, fearing that effort or facing setbacks may expose their supposed deficiencies.

In contrast, the *growth mindset* is based on the belief that our abilities and intelligence can be developed through dedication, effort, and a willingness to learn. People with a growth mindset view challenges as opportunities for growth, failures as stepping-stones toward success, and effort as the key to progress. They understand that talents can be nurtured, skills can be honed, and intelligence can be expanded through deliberate practice and a belief in their potential for growth.

The Power of Mindset

Research by psychologists like Carol Dweck has shown that our mindset profoundly impacts our achievements, relationships, and our overall existence. The mindset we adopt influences our motivation, resilience, and willingness to take on new challenges. It shapes how we respond to setbacks, criticism, and adversity. By understanding the differences between a fixed and a growth mindset, we can unlock the power to transform our lives and tap into our true potential.

A study by Lisa S. Blackwell and her team explored the impact of teaching a growth mindset to students.

The researchers found that students taught about the malleability of intelligence and the potential for growth performed better academically than those not exposed to this mindset intervention (Blackwell, Trzesniewski, & Dweck, 2007). This study demonstrates the potential for mindset interventions to enhance learning outcomes and foster a positive attitude toward challenges and growth.

Getting Rid of a Fixed Mindset

Recognizing the limitations of a fixed mindset, we can embark on a journey of transformation to cultivate a growth mindset within ourselves. We explore practical strategies to break free from the constraints of a fixed mindset and nurture a mindset of growth and possibility.

These strategies include:

- **Embracing Self-Awareness**: The first step towards shifting from a fixed mindset to a growth mindset is to become aware of our own fixed beliefs and thought patterns. By recognizing when we are operating from a fixed mindset, we can consciously challenge and reframe those beliefs.

- **ChallengingLimiting Beliefs**: Identify and challenge the limiting beliefs that hold you back. Examine the negative self-talk and assumptions that reinforce a fixed mindset and consciously replace them with positive, growth-oriented beliefs.

- **Embracing Failure as a Learning Opportunity**:

Instead of fearing failure, view it as a natural part of the learning process. Understand that failure provides valuable lessons and opportunities for growth. Embrace a mindset that allows you to learn from mistakes and setbacks, using them as stepping-stones to future success.

- **Cultivating a Growth Mindset Identity:** Develop an identity rooted in a growth mindset. Affirm your belief in your capacity for growth and improvement. Focus on the process of learning and development rather than solely on outcomes or external validation.

- **Embracing Continuous Learning:** Cultivate a thirst for knowledge and a curiosity about the world around you. Embrace challenges and seek opportunities to expand your skills and knowledge. Emphasize the journey of growth and the joy of learning rather than fixating on immediate results.

By consciously practicing these strategies, we can gradually release the grip of a fixed mindset and embrace the transformative power of a growth mindset. The journey of cultivating a growth mindset has just begun. Delving deeper into these practical tools, strategies, and insights will guide us on this transformative path.

Part 2: Nurturing a Growth Mindset—The Key to Unlocking Potential

The power of a mindset and its transformative impact changes the trajectory of our lives. We have explored the power of mindset and its transformative impact on our lives. Now, we dive deeper into the practical steps and strategies for nurturing and cultivating a growth mindset. We understand that embracing a growth mindset is not a one-time event but an ongoing process of self-discovery and personal development. By immersing ourselves in the principles and practices outlined in this chapter, we can unlock our true potential and create a mindset that fuels our growth and success.

Embracing a Growth Mindset in Daily Life

We begin by exploring how we can integrate a growth mindset into our daily lives. From the moment we wake up to the time we go to bed, there are numerous opportunities to foster a growth mindset. We delve into the power of positive self-talk and affirmations, the importance of embracing challenges and seeking feedback, and the significance of setting growth-oriented goals. By intentionally infusing a growth mindset into our thoughts, actions, and interactions, we create a foundation for continuous growth and development.

The Role of Effort and Practice

One of the fundamental tenets of a growth mindset is the understanding that effort and practice are essential for growth and mastery. We will examine deliberate practice, emphasizing the importance of consistent, purposeful, and focused effort in achieving excellence. Through real-life examples of renowned individuals who have harnessed the power of effort and practice, we understand that talent alone is not enough; the combination of talent, effort, and a growth mindset leads to true mastery.

Embracing Challenges and Overcoming Obstacles

In this section, we explore the significance of embracing challenges and overcoming obstacles in our journey of growth. We discuss the concept of a "challenge mindset" and the importance of stepping outside our comfort zones to expand our capabilities. We highlight the transformative power of resilience and perseverance, sharing stories of individuals who have faced adversity with courage and determination. We unlock our resilience and tenacity by viewing challenges as opportunities for growth and embracing a mindset of continuous improvement.

Cultivating a Love for Learning

A growth mindset is deeply intertwined with a love for learning. This section explores how we can cultivate and nurture a lifelong love for learning. We delve into the importance of curiosity, open-mindedness, and intellectual humility. We discuss strategies for expanding our knowledge, such as seeking new experiences, exploring diverse perspectives, and engaging in continuous learning opportunities. By embracing a love for learning, we foster a growth mindset that propels us toward personal and professional growth.

Building Resilience in the Face of Setbacks

No growth journey is without setbacks and failures. In this section, we explore the vital role of resilience in overcoming setbacks and bouncing back stronger. We discuss strategies for building resilience, such as reframing setbacks as learning opportunities, cultivating self-compassion, seeking support from others, and practicing mindfulness. By embracing a growth mindset, we develop the resilience to navigate through adversity, learn from failures, and emerge stronger and more determined on our path to success.

Fostering a Growth Mindset in Others

Finally, we delve into the importance of fostering a growth mindset in others. We recognize that as we embrace a growth mindset, we can inspire and uplift those around us. We explore the role of effective communication, providing constructive feedback, and cultivating a supportive environment that encourages growth and fosters a belief in the potential of others. We create an environment that fuels collective growth and success by nurturing a growth mindset in our communities, organizations, and relationships. With a growth mindset, we embrace challenges as opportunities, view effort as a stepping-stone to mastery, and cultivate a love for learning that propels us toward our full potential. As we continue our journey, the subsequent chapters will delve deeper into specific areas where a growth mindset can be applied, empowering us to unleash our potential in all aspects of our lives.

As we conclude this chapter, we invite all readers to reflect on their own mindset and its profound influence on their lives. We recognize that embracing a growth mindset is a continuous journey that requires dedication, self-reflection, and intentional practice. By integrating the principles and strategies outlined in this chapter into our daily lives, we unlock the transformative power of a growth mindset.

With a growth mindset, we embrace challenges as opportunities, view effort as a stepping-stone to mastery, and cultivate a love for learning that propels us toward our full potential. The subsequent chapters will delve deeper into specific areas where a growth mindset can be applied, empowering us to unleash our potential in all aspects of our lives. We are called to examine our beliefs, challenge our assumptions, and embrace the potential for growth and transformation.

In the upcoming chapters, we will do a deep dive into the characteristics and consequences of fixed and growth mindsets. We will also explore the origins and influences of these mindsets, examining how they affect various aspects of our lives, such as education, work, relationships, and personal development. Additionally, we will uncover practical strategies and techniques to shift from a fixed mindset to a growth mindset.

Chapter 2

The Fixed Mindset

Now that we have explored the concept of mindsets and introduced the fixed and growth mindsets, let's go deeper into the fixed mindset, understanding its characteristics, origins, and impact on personal development and achievement.

Characteristics of the Fixed Mindset

The fixed mindset is characterized by specific beliefs and behaviors that shape our approach to challenges, setbacks, and our own abilities. Here are some key characteristics of the fixed mindset:

- **Belief in Fixed Traits:** Individuals with a fixed mindset believe that their qualities, such as intelligence, talent, and abilities, are fixed traits that cannot be significantly changed or developed. They perceive these traits as inherent and unchangeable.

- **Fear of Failure:** People with a fixed mindset tend to fear failure and see it as a reflection of their own inadequacy. They often avoid challenges that might expose their perceived deficiencies, preferring to stay within their comfort zones.

- **Avoidance of Effort**: Individuals with a fixed mind-set often avoid putting in significant effort, as they believe that their abilities are fixed and that effort is unnecessary. They seek to demonstrate their abilities effortlessly, seeking validation through their natural talents.

- **Negative Response to Criticism**: Those with a fixed mindset may respond defensively to criticism or feedback. They may perceive it as a personal attack rather than an opportunity for growth, leading to resistance and defensiveness.

Origins and Influences of the Fixed Mindset

The development of a fixed mindset can be influenced by various factors, including:

- **Childhood Experiences**: Messages received during childhood, such as excessive focus on innate abilities or being labeled as "smart" or "talented," can contribute to developing a fixed mindset. Praise for outcomes rather than effort can also reinforce a fixed mindset.

- **Cultural and Social Influences:** Cultural values, societal expectations, and peer influences can shape the mindset individuals adopt. Environments emphasizing natural talents over growth and effort can reinforce the fixed mindset.

- **Previous Setbacks and Failures**: Experiences of failure or setbacks can impact one's mindset. Repeated failures without proper support or a growth-oriented perspective can lead individuals to develop a fixed mindset as a defense mechanism.

Impact of the Fixed Mindset

The fixed mindset can have significant consequences for personal development and achievement. Some of the impacts include:

- **Stagnation:** The belief in fixed traits can lead to a lack of motivation to learn, grow, and take on new challenges. Individuals may become stagnant, limiting their potential for personal and professional development.

- **Avoidance of Challenges:** Fear of failure and a desire to maintain a positive self-image can lead individuals with a fixed mindset to avoid challenges that may stretch their abilities. This avoidance hinders their growth and limits their opportunities for success.

- **Difficulty with Resilience:** Individuals with a fixed mindset may struggle to bounce back when faced with setbacks or obstacles. They may interpret failures as permanent and indicative of their limitations, hindering their ability to persevere and overcome challenges.

- **Reduced Capacity for Learning:** The fixed mindset can create a barrier to learning and embracing new knowledge and skills. The belief that abilities are fixed limits the willingness to invest effort in learning and may lead to a narrow and rigid view of one's capabilities.

Understanding the characteristics and consequences of a fixed mindset is essential for personal growth and development. In the next chapter, we will explore the alternative mindset—the growth mindset—and how it differs from the fixed mindset. By recognizing the limitations of a fixed mindset, we can begin the journey toward embracing a growth mindset and unlocking our full potential.

My Story

As a child, I was full of boundless imagination and dreams, but life circumstances gradually dimmed that light within me. Growing up in a challenging environment where dreams were considered impractical and unrealistic, I learned to suppress my aspirations and conform to the limited expectations set by others. The joy of dreaming faded, and a fixed mindset took root. The fear of failure and the belief that my abilities were fixed and unchangeable plagued me. One day I realized that this kind of thinking was sucking every bit of desire for life out of me. I thought, "If I am going to live beyond this moment, something has got to change."

I knew that I had to immerse myself in personal growth. As I did this, my perception and perspective of myself started to change, and my relationships also began to flourish. I surrounded myself with individuals who shared my growth-oriented mind-set, forming a supportive network that uplifted and encouraged me to pursue my dreams fearlessly.

Today, I stand here as a testament to the transforma-tive power of a growth mindset. I understand that dreams are not meant to be fantasies but the seeds of possibility. When nurtured with dedication and belief, they blossom into a future filled with growth, fulfill-ment, and the joy of living a life aligned with true potential fueled by purpose.

Chapter 3

The Growth Mindset

Previously, we explored the fixed mindset's character-istics, origins, and impacts. So, we'll shift our focus to the growth mindset now—a mindset that empowers individuals to embrace challenges, persevere through setbacks, and unlock their potential for growth and achievement.

Understanding the Growth Mindset

The growth mindset is grounded in the belief that our abilities, intelligence, and talents can be devel-oped through effort, learning, and dedication. It is the understanding that our potential is not predeter-mined but malleable and expandable. Here are some key aspects of the growth mindset:

- **Embracing Challenges**: Individuals with a growth mindset see challenges as opportunities for growth and learning. They view difficulties as a chance to develop new skills, expand their knowledge, and enhance their capabilities. Instead of avoiding challenges, they actively seek them out, knowing they can overcome obstacles and achieve success through effort and perseverance.

- **Cultivating Resilience**: Resilience is a fundamental

trait associated with the growth mindset. People with a growth mindset understand that setbacks and failures are part of the learning process. They don't let setbacks define them or deter their progress. Instead, they bounce back, learn from their mistakes, and use them as stepping-stones toward future achievements.

- **Value of Effort and Persistence**: Effort is a necessary component of growth and achievement in the growth mindset. Individuals with this mindset understand that true mastery and improvement require sustained effort and deliberate practice. They embrace the idea that hard work, dedication, and perseverance are crucial for realizing their goals.

- **Embracing Learning and Feedback**: A growth mindset fosters a love for learning and a desire to expand knowledge and skills continually. Individuals actively seek out feedback and view it as valuable information for improvement. They understand that feedback helps identify areas of growth and refine their approach, ultimately leading to greater success.

- **Nurturing a Positive View of Others' Success**: People with a growth mindset are inspired by the success of others. Instead of feeling threatened or envious, they see others' achievements as proof that growth and progress are attainable. They celebrate others' successes and use them as motivation for their own growth journey.

- **Embracing Change:** The growth mindset embraces change as an opportunity for personal growth. It welcomes new experiences, perspectives, and challenges. Individuals with a growth mindset understand that change fosters adaptability, resilience, and continuous improvement.

Benefits of the Growth Mindset

The growth mindset offers numerous benefits for personal development and achievement, including:

- **Increased Motivation:** The belief in the potential for growth and improvement fuels intrinsic motivation, enabling individuals to take on challenges and persist in the face of adversity.

- **Resilience and Adaptability:** With a growth mindset, individuals develop resilience and adaptability, allowing them to navigate obstacles, setbacks, and changes more effectively.

- **Expansion of Skills and Abilities:** The growth mindset encourages continuous learning and deliberate practice, leading to the development and expansion of skills, knowledge, and abilities.

- **Fulfillment and Satisfaction:** Embracing the growth mindset leads to a sense of fulfillment and satisfaction as individuals witness their progress and achievements through their efforts.

The growth mindset empowers individuals to embrace challenges, cultivate resilience, value effort and persistence, embrace learning and feedback, nurture positive perspectives on success, and embrace change. In the following chapters, we will explore how to cultivate and apply the growth mindset in various aspects of life, including education, the workplace, relationships, and personal development. By embracing the growth mindset, we can unlock our potential for continuous growth, achievement, and personal fulfillment.

Chapter 4

Nurturing a Growth Mindset in Education

Education plays a vital role in shaping mindsets and providing opportunities for personal growth. This chapter will explore how the growth mindset can be nurtured in educational settings. We will discuss the importance of embracing challenges, developing resilience, and fostering a love for learning to cultivate a growth mindset among students.

Embracing Challenges

In a growth mindset-oriented education, challenges are seen as opportunities for growth and development. Teachers and educators can encourage students to tackle challenging tasks, assignments, and projects that stretch their abilities. By creating a supportive environment that emphasizes effort and improvement rather than just outcomes, students can develop a belief in their capacity to learn and overcome obstacles.

Developing Resilience

Resilience is a critical skill for students to navigate the ups and downs of their educational journey. Educators can foster resilience by teaching students to embrace failure as a stepping-stone toward success.

Encouraging reflection, providing constructive feedback, and helping students learn from their mistakes allow them to bounce back stronger, develop the mindset that setbacks are temporary, and provide valuable learning opportunities.

Fostering a Love for Learning

A growth mindset in education promotes a love for learning and a thirst for knowledge. Educators can inspire students by connecting the curriculum to real-life applications, showing the relevance of what they are learning. By emphasizing the joy of discovery, encouraging curiosity, and providing opportunities for independent exploration, educators can instill a lifelong passion for learning within students.

Effort and Perseverance

In a growth mindset-oriented classroom, effort and perseverance are celebrated and valued. Educators can provide specific and constructive feedback that focuses on the process and effort rather than solely on outcomes. By acknowledging students' hard work and progress, educators reinforce the idea that growth comes through effort and determination, fostering a belief that they can overcome challenges with persistence.

Creating a Supportive Learning Environment:

To nurture a growth mindset, creating a supportive learning environment is essential. Educators can establish a safe space where all learners feel comfortable taking risks, sharing their ideas, and making mistakes. By promoting collaboration, cooperation, and positive peer interactions, students can learn from one another and develop a sense of collective growth.

Teaching the Power of Yet

Encouraging a growth mindset involves teaching students to embrace the phrase "I can't do it...yet." By emphasizing that abilities can be developed over time, teachers can help students see challenges as opportunities for growth. Encouraging a "yet" mindset reframes failures or difficulties as temporary setbacks on the path to mastery, promoting perseverance and resilience.

Promoting Growth Mindset Language

Educators can incorporate growth mindset language into their teaching practices. Encouraging learners to use phrases like "I will give it another try," "I haven't mastered it yet," or "I can learn from this" promotes a growth mindset. By modeling and reinforcing growth-oriented language, educators help students develop a positive internal dialogue and approach challenges with a growth mindset.

In conclusion, nurturing a growth mindset in education is a powerful way to empower students and unlock their full potential. By embracing challenges, developing resilience, fostering a love for learning, valuing effort and perseverance, creating a supportive learning environment, teaching the power of yet, and promoting growth mindset language, educators can cultivate a growth mindset among students. This enhances their academic success and equips them with essential skills and attitudes for lifelong learning and personal growth.

Chapter 5

Developing a Growth Mindset in the Workplace

The growth mindset is not limited to educational settings; it is also highly applicable in the workplace. In this chapter, we will explore how individuals can cultivate a growth mindset in their professional lives. We will discuss the importance of embracing challenges, fostering a culture of learning and feedback, and developing resilience to unlock personal and professional growth.

Embracing Challenges

Challenges in the workplace provide opportunities for growth and development. Individuals with a growth mindset see challenges as pathways to success rather than insurmountable obstacles. They actively seek out new and challenging tasks, knowing they can expand their skills and abilities through effort and learning. By embracing challenges, individuals can continuously improve their performance and reach new heights in their careers.

Alex, a young entrepreneur, faced a significant setback in his business when a crucial client of his pulled out of a major deal. His fixed mindset almost caused him to give up, believing his lack of ability was to blame. However, Alex shifted to a growth mindset with the support of a mindset coach and a mentor. He embraced the setback as a learning opportunity, sought feedback, and worked on improving his skills and strategies. With perseverance and a belief in his capacity for growth, Alex turned the catastrophe into a catalyst for innovation and success, propelling his business to new heights and inspiring others on the power of a growth mindset.

Fostering a Culture of Learning

Organizations that foster a culture of learning provide an environment where individuals are encouraged to acquire new knowledge and develop new skills. This includes providing access to training programs, workshops, and educational resources. Leaders and managers play a crucial role in creating a culture that values continuous learning and supports employees' growth and development.

Encouraging Feedback and Reflection

A growth mindset in the workplace involves valuing feedback as a tool for growth and improvement. Employees should be encouraged to seek feedback from their peers, managers, and mentors, viewing it as an opportunity to learn and develop. Constructive feedback helps individuals identify areas for growth and refine their skills.

Regular reflection and self-assessment also contribute to personal and professional growth.

Building Resilience

Resilience is vital in the workplace, as individuals encounter setbacks, failures, and demanding situations. A growth mindset fosters resilience by teaching individuals to view setbacks as learning experiences and stepping-stones toward success. Resilient individuals bounce back from challenges, adapt to change, and remain motivated and focused on their goals.

Promoting a Growth Mindset in Leadership

Leaders have a significant impact on shaping the mindset culture within organizations. Leaders should model a growth mindset by being open to learning, embracing challenges, and accepting feedback. They can encourage their teams to adopt a growth mindset by recognizing effort, providing constructive feedback, and fostering a supportive environment where individuals can take risks and learn from their experiences.

Supporting Professional Development

Investing in professional development opportunities is essential for fostering a growth mindset in the workplace. Organizations can provide employees access to training programs, mentorship initiatives, and opportunities to take on new responsibilities. By supporting employees' professional growth, organizations demonstrate their commitment to their employees' development and encourage a mindset of continuous improvement.

Embracing Innovation and Change

In a growth mindset workplace, individuals are open to innovation and change. They see change as an opportunity for growth and improvement rather than something to be feared or resisted. Employees are encouraged to think creatively, adapt to new technologies and methodologies, and embrace change as a catalyst for progress.

In summary, developing a growth mindset in the workplace is essential for personal and professional growth. Individuals and organizations can unlock their full potential by embracing challenges, fostering a culture of learning and feedback, building resilience, promoting a growth mindset in leadership, supporting professional development, and embracing innovation and change. Cultivating a growth mindset in the workplace leads to increased motivation, higher job satisfaction, and enhanced creativity and productivity, ultimately contributing to individual and organizational success.

Chapter 6

Relationships and the Growth Mindset

The Story of Serena and John

A couple that seemed inseparable found themselves at a crossroads in their relationship. The daily grind had taken a toll on their connection, leaving them feeling distant, unfulfilled, and like they had reached a plateau. Feeling desperate to salvage what they had, they sought guidance from a coach-mentor. With compassionate guidance, I helped them see that their individual mindsets and perspectives were blocking them from growing the love they once shared.

The growth mindset extends beyond individual development and is crucial in fostering healthy and thriving relationships. This chapter will explore how the growth mindset can enhance personal or professional relationships. We will discuss effective communication, embracing challenges together, and nurturing a growth-oriented perspective in relationships.

The Power of Effective Communication

Effective communication is the foundation of healthy relationships. In a growth mindset-oriented relationship, open and honest communication is encouraged.

Individuals express their thoughts, feelings, and needs while actively listening to others. They strive to understand different perspectives and engage in constructive dialogue, fostering mutual respect and understanding.

Embracing Challenges Together

In growth mindset relationships, both parties embrace challenges as opportunities for growth and learning. They support each other in setting and pursuing shared goals, recognizing that setbacks and failures are natural parts of the journey. By facing challenges together, individuals strengthen their bond and encourage one another to persevere and grow.

Constructive Feedback and Growth

Feedback in growth mindset relastionships is viewed as a means for growth and improvement. Individuals provide constructive feedback to each other, focusing on specific behaviors or actions rather than personal attacks. They value feedback as an opportunity for self-reflection and personal development, fostering a culture of continuous improvement within the relationship.

Nurturing Positive Mindset in Conflict Resolution

Conflicts are inevitable in relationships, but a growth mindset can transform how conflicts are approached and resolved. Individuals in growth mindset relationships see conflicts as opportunities for deeper understanding and growth. They engage in respectful and constructive discussions, seeking mutually beneficial resolutions that promote personal and relationship development.

Supporting Each Other's Growth

In growth mindset relationships, individuals actively support and encourage each other's personal growth and development. They celebrate each other's achievements, providing encouragement and reinforcement. They understand that personal growth is not a competition but a collaborative journey where both parties can thrive.

Cultivating Empathy and Understanding

Empathy and understanding are essential elements of growth mindset relationships. Individuals with a growth mindset strive to understand each other's perspectives, experiences, and challenges. They cultivate empathy, recognizing that everyone has their own unique journey and struggles. This empathy fosters compassion and strengthens the bond within the relationship.

Nurturing a growth mindset in relationships is crucial for personal and interpersonal growth. Individuals can cultivate thriving and fulfilling relationships by embracing challenges, practicing effective communication, providing constructive feedback, and fostering empathy and understanding. When we approach relationships with a growth mindset, we create an environment that encourages growth, resilience, and open-mindedness. We recognize that challenges and conflicts are opportunities for learning and understanding rather than threats to the relationship.

Communicating openly and honestly builds trust and creates a safe space for vulnerability and growth. We value feedback as a means for improvement and view it as an opportunity to deepen our understanding of ourselves and others. Embracing a growth mindset in relationships also means celebrating the successes and growth of our partners, friends, or colleagues. We understand that their achievements do not diminish our own but inspire us to strive for growth and development.

Moreover, cultivating empathy and understanding fosters deeper connections and creates a supportive network where individuals can thrive. We embrace the diversity of experiences and perspectives, recognizing that it enriches our growth journey. It is important to remember that developing a growth mindset in relationships is an ongoing process. It requires continuous effort, self-reflection, and a willingness to learn and adapt. By nurturing a growth mindset in our relationships, we contribute to our personal growth and create a positive ripple effect that extends to those around us.

As we embrace the principles of a growth mindset in our relationships, we empower ourselves and others to face challenges with resilience, communicate effectively, and foster a sense of unity and growth. By cultivating a growth mindset in our relationships, we create a supportive and nurturing environment where individuals can thrive, learn from one another, and achieve their fullest potential.

So, whatever became of Serena and John? Through self-reflection, clarity, and open dialogue, Serena and John realized the need to shift their perspectives and be more understanding of each other's needs. They learned to communicate empathetically and embrace a growth mindset with my support. As they navigated this journey together, their love for each other grew, and they found solace in realizing they held the power to save their relationship. Through practicing the techniques, they learned Serena and John discovered a renewed sense of hope and a deep connection that illuminated their path to a more fulfilling future.

Chapter 7

The Power of Beliefs and Mindset Shifts

Beliefs and mindset are pivotal in shaping our lives and influencing our choices and actions. This chapter will explore the power of beliefs and mindset shifts in cultivating a growth-oriented perspective. We will examine the influence of beliefs on mindset and strategies for challenging and transforming limiting beliefs.

The Influence of Beliefs on Mindset

Beliefs act as lenses through which we view ourselves and the world around us. Our beliefs about our abilities, potential, and the nature of intelligence shape our mindset. Understanding the influence of beliefs is vital to unlocking the power of mindset shifts and personal growth.

Challenging Limiting Beliefs

Limiting beliefs are self-imposed barriers that hinder our growth and potential. We must identify and challenge these limiting beliefs to cultivate a growth mindset. By questioning the validity of these beliefs and seeking evidence to the contrary, we can shift our mindset and open ourselves up to new possibilities.

Strategies for Mindset Shifts

Mindset shifts require intentional effort and practice. Here are some strategies to facilitate a mindset shift from fixed to growth:

- **Awareness and Self-Reflection**: Developing self-awareness allows us to recognize our fixed mindset tendencies and understand their impact on our lives. Regular self-reflection helps us identify limiting beliefs and patterns that hold us back.

- **Cultivating a Growth Mindset Language**: Language shapes our thoughts and beliefs. By intentionally using growth mindset language, such as affirming our potential for growth, embracing challenges, and focusing on effort and learning, we can rewire our thinking patterns and reinforce a growth mindset.

- **Embracing New Experiences and Taking Risks**: Stepping out of our comfort zones and embracing new experiences helps us challenge our limiting beliefs. Taking calculated risks allows us to push past our perceived limitations and discover new capabilities.

- **Surround Yourself with Growth Mindset Supporters**: Building a network of individuals who embody and encourage a growth mindset can greatly support our own mindset shift. Seek mentors, coaches, or like-minded individuals who inspire and motivate you to embrace growth and challenge your beliefs.

- **Celebrating Progress and Small Wins**: Acknowledging and celebrating our progress, no matter how small, reinforces the belief in our ability to grow. By Celebrating Progress and Small Wins: Acknowledging and celebrating our progress, no matter how small, reinforces the belief in our ability to grow. By recognizing and appreciating our efforts and achievements along the way, we build momentum and confidence in our capacity for growth.

- **Embracing Continuous Learning:** Adopting a lifelong learning mindset nurtures a growth-oriented perspective. Actively seeking new knowledge, pursuing personal and professional development opportunities, and staying curious keep our minds open to growth and change.

Beliefs and mindset shape our perception of ourselves and our world. By challenging and transforming limiting beliefs, intentionally shifting our mindset, and embracing a growth-oriented perspective, we can unlock our true potential and embrace a life of continuous growth and personal development. Mindset shifts require dedication, self-reflection, and consistent practice, but the rewards of adopting a growth mindset are limitless.

Chapter 8

Parenting and Teaching with a Growth Mindset

Parenting and teaching play a significant role in shaping children's mindsets and fostering their growth and development. This chapter will explore how parents and educators can cultivate a growth mindset in children and students. We will discuss strategies for providing feedback, encouraging effort and resilience, and creating a nurturing environment that promotes a growth mindset.

Nurturing a Growth Mindset in Children

- **Encouraging Effort and Process**: Emphasize the value of effort, hard work, and perseverance in achieving success. Praise children for their effort, strategies, and progress rather than solely focusing on outcomes. Teach them that mistakes and failures are opportunities for learning and growth.

- **Teaching the Power of "Yet"**: Introduce the concept of "yet" to children, teaching them that they may not have mastered a skill or concept yet, but with effort and practice, they can improve over time. This instills a growth mindset and helps them embrace challenges without feeling discouraged by initial setbacks.

- **Providing Constructive Feedback**: Offer specific, constructive feedback that focuses on the process and effort rather than making judgments about their abilities. Encourage children to reflect on their strengths and areas for growth and support them in setting realistic goals to improve continuously.

- **Modeling a Growth Mindset**: Demonstrate a growth mindset through your actions and language. Share stories of your challenges and failures and how you persevered and learned from them. By being a role model, you inspire children to adopt a growth mindset in their own lives.

Fostering a Growth Mindset in Education

- **Creating a Safe and Supportive Learning Environment**: Establish a classroom or learning environment where students feel safe to take risks, make mistakes, and ask questions. Encourage student collaboration, cooperation, and support to foster a growth mindset.

- **Teaching the Value of Reflection**: Incorporate reflection activities into the learning process, encouraging students to assess their progress, strengths, and areas for improvement. Guide them in setting meaningful goals and help them develop strategies to achieve them.

- **Providing Growth-Focused Feedback**: Offer feedback highlighting specific efforts, progress, and areas for growth. Avoid labeling or categorizing students based on their abilities or intelligence. Instead, emphasize the importance of continuous improvement and the belief in their potential to develop and succeed.

- **Cultivating a Love for Learning**: Foster a passion for learning by making lessons engaging, relevant, and connected to real-life experiences. Encourage curiosity, exploration, and critical thinking, instilling in students a desire to seek knowledge and develop a lifelong love for learning.

Embracing success with a growth mindset is a transformative journey that requires a shift in perspective and a commitment to continuous improvement. Throughout this chapter, we have explored the power of leveraging achievements with a growth mindset and embracing lifelong learning. We have learned that success is not merely reaching a specific destination but rather a series of milestones in an ongoing journey of growth. By celebrating our achievements, big and small, we reinforce the belief in our ability to succeed and inspire ourselves to keep pushing forward.

Leveraging achievements with a growth mindset involves recognizing our progress, the skills we have developed, and the lessons we have learned along the way. It is about acknowledging the effort, perseverance, and resilience that have led to our accomplishments. At the same time, embracing continuous improvement and lifelong learning ensures that success becomes a springboard for future growth. It is about staying curious, seeking new knowledge and experiences, and challenging ourselves to reach new heights. By engaging in continuous learning, we remain adaptable, innovative, and ready to embrace the opportunities that come our way.

Throughout this chapter, we have explored strategies for embracing success with a growth mindset. We have learned the importance of setting realistic goals, celebrating milestones, and maintaining a positive perspective. We have seen the power of self-reflection in tracking our progress and identifying areas for further growth. As we conclude this chapter, let us remember that embracing success with a growth mindset is not a destination but a lifelong journey. It requires resilience, a willingness to learn from both successes and failures and a commitment to personal growth. By integrating the principles and strategies discussed in this chapter into our lives, we can unlock our true potential and create a path toward continued success and fulfillment. Embracing a growth mindset allows us to navigate challenges gracefully, persevere through setbacks, and continually expand our capabilities.

Chapter 9

Sustaining a Growth Mindset

Developing a growth mindset is an ongoing journey that requires consistent effort and nurturing. This chapter explores strategies for sustaining a growth mindset in various aspects of life. We will discuss maintaining resilience, overcoming setbacks, and creating a supportive environment that reinforces and sustains a growth mindset.

Maintaining Resilience

- Embracing Self-Compassion: Cultivate self-compassion by treating yourself with kindness and understanding when faced with challenges or setbacks. Practice self-care and acknowledge that setbacks are part of the growth process, allowing yourself to bounce back stronger.

- Reframing Setbacks as Learning Opportunities: View setbacks as valuable learning experiences rather than failures. Seek lessons and insights from setbacks, identifying areas for growth and improvement. Embrace a solution-focused mindset that sees challenges as opportunities to make the proper steps toward success.

- Setting Realistic Goals: Establish realistic goals that

are challenging yet achievable. Break down large goals into smaller, manageable steps. Celebrate progress along the way, recognizing the effort and ng to podcasts or TED Talks, attending workshops, or participating in online courses that promote personal growth and mindset development.

- Journaling and Reflection: Set aside time for intro-spection and journaling. Reflect on your growth journey, milestones achieved, challenges over-come, and lessons learned. This self-reflection aids in maintaining perspective, tracking progress, and identifying areas for further growth.

Sustaining a growth mindset requires consistent effort and the support of a nurturing environment. You can sustain and strengthen your growth mindset by main-taining resilience, reframing setbacks, and setting realistic goals. Surround yourself with growth mind-set supporters who cultivate positive relationships with healthy practicing of mindset maintenance. Inte-grating these strategies into your life will aid you in embracing challenges and persevering through obsta-cles. These repetitive practices will unlock your true potential for continuous growth and achievement.

Chapter 10

Embracing Success with a Growth Mindset

In our journey of cultivating a growth mindset, it is crucial to understand how to embrace success. This chapter will explore the significance of a growth mindset in achieving personal and professional goals. We will discuss strategies for celebrating achievements, maintaining a growth-oriented perspective, and continuing growth and learning.

Leveraging Achievements with a Growth Mindset

- **Recognizing and Celebrating Progress**: Acknowledge and celebrate your achievements, no matter how big or small. Reflect on the growth and effort that led to those accomplishments. By recognizing your progress, you reinforce the belief in your ability to succeed and motivate yourself to continue pushing forward.

- **Embracing a Growth-Oriented Perspective:** Rather than viewing success as a destination, see it as a milestone in your ongoing growth journey. Embrace the mindset that there is always room for further improvement and learning, even after achieving significant milestones. This perspective fosters continuous growth and prevents complacency.

- **Cultivating a Sense of Gratitude:** Express gratitude for the opportunities, resources, and support that contributed to your success. Recognize the role that others have played in your achievements and show appreciation for their contributions. Gratitude cultivates humility and a sense of interconnectedness, allowing for continued growth and collaboration.

- **Reflecting on Lessons Learned:** Take time to reflect on the lessons learned throughout your journey to success. Identify the strategies, skills, and mindset shifts that have contributed to your achievements. By understanding what has worked for you, you can apply these insights to future endeavors and continue to grow.

Embracing Continuous Improvement and Lifelong Learning

- **Embracing a Growth-Oriented Identity**: Foster a growth-oriented identity that sees success as a result of continuous improvement and effort. Embrace the belief that abilities can be developed and refined over time. By adopting this identity, you free yourself from the pressure of perfection and empower yourself to embrace challenges and take risks.

- **Seeking New Challenges**: Challenge yourself to

step outside your comfort zone and tackle new and ambitious goals. Embrace the mindset that challenges are opportunities for growth and expansion. By consistently seeking new challenges, you continue to push the boundaries of your abilities and achieve even greater success.

- **Engaging in Lifelong Learning**: Commit to lifelong learning and personal development. Stay curious, seek out new knowledge, and embrace opportunities for growth. This can include attending workshops, conferences, or seminars, pursuing advanced education, or engaging in self-study. Continuously expanding your skills and knowledge keeps you adaptable and prepared for future success.

- **Supporting Others' Growth**: Share your knowledge, experiences, and insights with others to support their growth journeys. Act as a mentor, coach, or role model, guiding and encouraging those striving for their own successes. By supporting others, you reinforce your own growth mindset and contribute to a culture of continuous improvement.

In conclusion, embracing success with a growth mindset is about recognizing and celebrating achievements while maintaining a perspective of continuous improvement and learning. By leveraging achievements, cultivating gratitude, reflecting on lessons learned, and embracing a growth-oriented identity, you can continue to thrive and achieve new heights. Embracing continuous improvement and lifelong learning ensures that success becomes a springboard for future growth and allows you to make a lasting impact on yourself and others. As you continue your growth journey, remember that the possibilities for personal and professional development are endless when approached with a growth mindset.

Chapter 11

The Necessity of Positive Reinforcement Statements and Affirmations in Building Growth Mindsets

The power of positive reinforcement statements and affirmations cannot be understated in our journey of developing a growth mindset. These tools are crucial in shaping our beliefs, boosting our confidence, and nurturing a growth-oriented perspective. This expanded chapter will explore the necessity of positive reinforcement statements and affirmations and discuss strategies for effectively incorporating them into our daily lives.

Understanding the Impact of Positive Reinforcement Statements: Positive reinforcement statements are affirmations and encouraging messages that focus on acknowledging and reinforcing our strengths, efforts, and progress. They are powerful tools for building and sustaining a growth mindset. Here are key reasons why positive reinforcement statements are necessary:

- **Shaping Beliefs**: Our beliefs play a significant role in how we perceive ourselves and our potential. Positive reinforcement statements challenge and reshape limiting beliefs by emphasizing our strengths and reinforcing our growth-oriented qualities. Over time, they help us develop a more positive and empowering self-perception.

- **Boosting Confidence and Motivation**: Positive reinforcement statements boost our confidence by reminding us of our capabilities and achievements. They provide motivation and encouragement to take on challenges, persevere through obstacles, and maintain a positive attitude. By reinforcing our self-belief, they inspire us to keep growing and striving for success.

- **Overcoming Self-Doubt and Fear**: Self-doubt and fear can be significant barriers to growth. Positive reinforcement statements counteract these negative emotions by instilling a sense of self-assurance and courage. They remind us that we have the capacity to learn, adapt, and overcome challenges, helping us push past our comfort zones and embrace new opportunities.

- **Fostering Resilience**: Resilience is crucial for navigating setbacks and failures. Positive reinforcement statements provide the reassurance and support needed to bounce back from setbacks. They remind us of our strengths, progress, and potential for growth, fostering a resilient mindset that enables us to persevere and learn from adversity.

Effective Strategies for Incorporating Positive Reinforcement Statements and Affirmations

- **Identify and Challenge Negative Self-Talk**: Become aware of negative self-talk and replace it with positive reinforcement statements. When you catch yourself engaging in self-doubt or self-criticism, intentionally counter it with a positive and empowering statement. For example, replace "I can't do it" with "I am capable of learning and improving with effort."

- **Personalize Affirmations to Your Goals and Values**: Tailor affirmations to align with your specific goals, values, and areas of growth. Craft statements that reflect your aspirations and remind you of your progress. For example, "I embrace challenges and view them as opportunities for growth."

- **Practice Daily Affirmation Rituals**: Dedicate time each day to affirmations. Repeat positive reinforcement statements aloud or write them down in a journal. Consistency is key, so integrate this practice into your daily routine to reinforce a growth mindset.

- **Visualize Success**: Combine positive reinforcement statements with visualization techniques. Visualize yourself successfully overcoming challenges and achieving your goals. Use affirmations to reinforce this visual imagery, such as "I see myself succeeding and growing with each step I take."

- **Seek Support and Accountability**: Share positive reinforcement statements with trusted friends, mentors, or family members who can support and hold you accountable. Create a supportive environment where you can exchange affirmations and encourage each other's growth mindset journeys.

Positive reinforcement statements and affirmations are essential for building and sustaining a growth mindset. They shape our beliefs, boost our confidence, foster resilience, and propel us toward continuous growth and success. By incorporating effective strategies such as identifying and challenging negative self-talk, personalizing affirmations, practicing daily affirmation rituals, visualizing success, and seeking support, we can harness the power of positive reinforcement statements to strengthen our growth mindset. Embrace the transformative impact of these affirmations and watch as they empower you to reach new heights, overcome challenges, and unlock your full potential.

Chapter 12

The Power of Gratitude and Unconditional Acceptance in Enhancing a Growth Mindset

Gratitude and unconditional acceptance are two powerful practices that complement and enhance the growth mindset. In this chapter, we will explore the profound impact of gratitude and unconditional acceptance on cultivating and strengthening a growth-oriented perspective. We will discuss the benefits of these practices and provide strategies for incorporating them into our lives.

The Power of Gratitude

Gratitude is the practice of recognizing and appreciating the positive aspects of our lives, including experiences, relationships, and personal growth. Here's how gratitude enhances a growth mindset:

- **Shifting Perspective**: Gratitude shifts our focus from what is lacking to what we have. It reframes challenges as opportunities for growth, helping us see the lessons and blessings within them. We develop a more optimistic and growth-oriented perspective by cultivating a grateful mindset.

- **Fostering Resilience**: Gratitude strengthens our

resilience by reminding us of the resources, support, and progress we have made. It helps us navigate setbacks and challenges with a positive attitude, knowing that we can overcome and learn from them.

- **Amplifying Positivity**: Expressing gratitude floods our minds with positive emotions, such as joy, contentment, and appreciation. These positive emotions fuel our motivation, creativity, and perseverance, enabling us to approach tasks and challenges with a growth-oriented mindset.

- **Cultivating Humility**: Gratitude fosters humility by recognizing that the support and contributions of others often influence our growth and achievements. It encourages us to acknowledge and value the efforts and impact of those around us, promoting collaboration and an openness to learning.

Unconditional Acceptance

Unconditional acceptance involves accepting yourself and others without judgment or conditions.

- **Embracing Imperfections**: Unconditional acceptance allows us to embrace our imperfections and see them as opportunities for growth. It liberates us from the fear of failure or making mistakes, fostering a growth-oriented mindset that encourages continuous learning and improvement.

- **Creating a Safe Environment**: Unconditional

acceptance fosters a safe and nurturing environment where individuals feel comfortable expressing their thoughts, ideas, and vulnerabilities. This safe space encourages risk-taking, creativity, and open communication, promoting growth and collaboration.

- **Embracing Diverse Perspectives**: Unconditional acceptance encourages us to value and appreciate diverse perspectives and experiences. It broadens our horizons, expands our understanding, and challenges our beliefs and assumptions. By embracing diverse perspectives, we foster a growth mindset that thrives on curiosity, learning, and embracing new ideas.

- **Encouraging Self-Compassion**: Unconditional acceptance includes extending compassion and understanding to ourselves. It helps us practice self-care, acknowledge our efforts, and be kind to ourselves when faced with challenges or setbacks. Self-compassion fuels resilience and motivates us to keep growing despite obstacles.

Incorporating Gratitude and Unconditional Acceptance into Daily Life

- **Gratitude Journaling**: Set aside time each day to reflect on and write down the things you are grateful for. Cultivate a habit of gratitude by focusing on both big and small moments of appreciation.

- **Acts of Kindness**: Practice acts of kindness towards

others as a way to express gratitude and promote a sense of unconditional acceptance. Engage in acts of generosity, support, or encouragement that contribute to the growth and well-being of others.

- **Mindful Reflection**: Regularly engage in mindfulness or meditation practices to cultivate a sense of gratitude and acceptance. Use these practices to deepen your self-awareness, acknowledge your emotions, and foster a non-judgmental attitude towards yourself and others.

- **Practice Empathy and Active Listening**: Develop empathy by actively listening to others without judgment or interruption. Seek to understand their perspectives, experiences, and challenges. Practice unconditional acceptance by validating their feelings and demonstrating empathy and understanding.

In conclusion, gratitude and unconditional acceptance are powerful practices that enhance and strengthen the growth mindset. By incorporating gratitude into our daily lives, we shift our perspective, foster resilience, amplify positivity, and cultivate humility. Unconditional acceptance promotes self-acceptance, creates a safe environment, encourages diverse perspectives, and fosters self-compassion.

As we integrate gratitude and unconditional acceptance into our mindset and interactions, we not only enhance our growth but also create an environment that nurtures and supports the growth of others. By embracing gratitude and unconditional acceptance, we deepen our commitment to lifelong learning, personal development, and the flourishing of ourselves and those around us.

Epilogue

In the journey of cultivating a growth mindset, we have explored the power of mindset, the importance of nurturing it in education and the workplace, its impact on relationships, and the role of beliefs and mindset shifts. We have delved into the necessity of positive reinforcement statements, affirmations, gratitude, and unconditional acceptance in fostering a growth-oriented perspective. We have also examined embracing success, sustaining a growth mindset, and navigating obstacles and change.

Throughout this book, we have discovered that mindset is not a fixed trait but a malleable quality that can be developed and nurtured. By shifting our perspective, embracing challenges, and fostering resilience, we have witnessed the transformative power of a growth mindset in various aspects of our lives.

We have learned that education is not just about knowledge acquisition but about instilling a love for learning, promoting effort and perseverance, and creating supportive environments that nurture growth mindsets in students and educators alike. In the workplace, we have seen how embracing a growth mindset drives innovation, encourages continuous learning, and fosters collaboration and adaptability.

Throughout this rendering, I have recognized the significant impact of my relationships on my growth journey. Effective communication, constructive feedback, empathy, and understanding are vital ingredients in nurturing growth mindsets in all interactions with others. Together, we can create supportive environments where everyone can thrive and embrace continuous growth.

Beliefs play a crucial role in shaping our mindset, and by challenging and shifting limiting beliefs, we open ourselves up to new possibilities and opportunities for growth. Positive reinforcement statements, affirmations, gratitude, and unconditional acceptance are powerful tools that shape our mindset, boost our confidence, and propel us toward personal and professional growth.

Embracing success with a growth mindset means celebrating achievements while maintaining a perspective of continuous improvement. We have learned that success is not a destination but a milestone in an ongoing journey of growth. We can sustain and strengthen our growth mindset by leveraging achievements, embracing continuous learning, and practicing self-reflection.

We have explored the importance of reflection, self-awareness, overcoming obstacles, and developing grit in nurturing a growth mindset. These qualities enable us to persevere through challenges, adapt to change, and thrive in an ever-evolving world.

As I conclude this book, it is essential to remember that developing and nurturing a growth mindset is ongoing. It requires dedication, self-reflection, and consistent effort. By embracing the principles and strategies shared throughout these pages, we unlock our true potential and embrace a life of continuous growth and personal development.

Each of us has the capacity to cultivate a growth mindset and embark on a transformative journey of self-discovery and achievement. Together, let us embrace the power of a growth mindset and create a world where possibilities are endless, resilience is unwavering, and growth is boundless.

May the wisdom and insights shared in this book inspire you to embrace the mindset for success, unlock your full potential, and positively impact your life and the lives of others all around!

Remember, the power to embrace growth resides within you. Embrace it with an open heart, an open mind, and a commitment to lifelong learning. The journey towards a growth mindset begins now.

With heartfelt gratitude,

Philip M. Baker

References

Blackwell, L. S., Trzesniewski, K. H., & Dweck, C. S. (2007). Implicit theories of intelligence predict achievement across an adolescent transition: A longitudinal study and an intervention. Child Development, 78(1), 246-263

Note: The reference page includes the key works and studies that have contributed to the research and understanding of mindsets, intelligence, and personal growth. These sources are referenced throughout the book *Unleashing Potential: Embracing the Power of a Growth Mindset* to provide credible and evidence-based insights.

About the Author

Philip M Baker is known for his compassionate and insightful approach to guiding others on their

Philip's mission is to empower individuals to embrace growth, navigate challenges with resilience, and create a life filled with purpose, joy, and personal fulfillment. He hopes his work will inspire others to embark on their transformative growth journey and unlock their true potential.

Philip is a musician and composer. He is also a renowned recording artist in the genre of smooth jazz and instrumental wellness music.

Philip is a father and is happily married to his wife, Deb.

Connect with Philip M. Baker:

Website: www.reimagininglifecoaches.com

Email: philip@reimagininglifecoaches

Social Media: Reimagininglifecoaches@instagram. com; facebook.com/philipmaurice

Made in the USA
Las Vegas, NV
25 January 2024

84848789R00046